GLOBAL
ECONOMICS

GLOBAL
ECONOMICS

Thomas O'Toole

Series Editor: M. Barbara Killen
Professor, University of Minnesota

 Lerner Publications Company ▪ Minneapolis, Minnesota

Library of Congress Cataloging-in-Publication Data

O'Toole, Thomas, 1941-
    Global economics / Thomas O'Toole.
        p.   cm. — (Economics for today)
    Summary: Explains various theories of economic development, discussing philosophical questions regarding the development of consumer cultures as a goal.
    ISBN 0-8225-1782-5
    1. Economic development—Juvenile literature. [1. Economic development.] I. Title.   II. Series.

HD75.8.086   1991
338.9dc20   90-34979
                                                                CIP
                                                                AC

Manufactured in the United States of America

1 2 3 4 5 6 7 8 9 10 00 99 98 97 96 95 94 93 92 91

CONTENTS

MOST OF THE WORLD

M ost people in the United States, Canada, western Europe, and Japan take so much for granted. Their daily lives are filled with comfort and convenience. Their houses are heated, their clothes are clean and comfortable, and they have more than enough food. They are entertained constantly by radio and television, and their cars, buses, or bicycles carry them to work, school, or vacation. In short, they are **affluent**.

But most people in the world are not affluent. The population

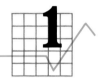

Children in industrialized countries, such as the United States, are often entertained by television.

of the world in 1990 was over 5 billion people. More than three-fourths of these people live in poverty-stricken countries. In fact, almost 800 million people could face starvation by the year 2000.

In the 1960s, '70s, and '80s, economists divided the world into three different groups of countries. The "First World" included **industrialized, market-economy**—or "capitalist"—countries, also referred to as the West. Countries such as the United States, Canada, Norway, Great Britain, and Japan were part of the First World. The "Second World" included countries with **centrally planned economies**—"communist" or "socialist" countries—such as the Soviet Union, China, and Cuba. The "Third World" included the poorer, nonindustrialized countries, most of which had recently been colonies of western countries. Most countries in South

America, central Africa, and Southeast Asia made up the Third World.

Recently, political change throughout the world has caused economists to define countries more on economic grounds alone, rather than economically and politically. They call the richer industrialized nations "developed" or "overdeveloped." Most of these countries are in the Northern Hemisphere, and are grouped together as the "North." Most of the poorer, nonindustrialized nations, which economists refer to as "less developed" or "underdeveloped," are south of the equator. They are grouped together as the "South."

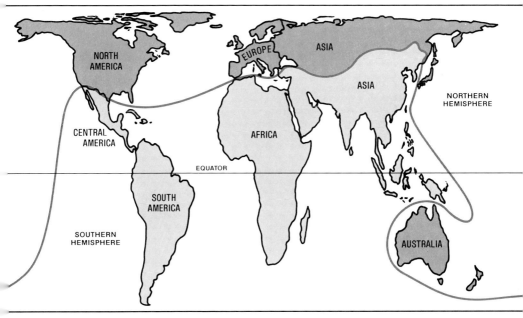

The world map—based on the less Eurocentric "Peter's Projection" of the world—shows that the majority of the industrialized countries lie in the Northern Hemisphere. Most of the less-developed countries lie in the Southern Hemisphere.

Case Study: The People of Croix Fer

To understand what life is like for the over 3 billion people who live in the poorer, southern countries, you can look at the people of Croix Fer—pronounced *Kwah Fair*—a village in Haiti near the border of the Dominican Republic. In many ways, the lives of the people of Croix Fer are similar to the lives of poor people in less-developed countries all over the world.

The economic lives of everyone in Croix Fer revolve around one fact—they are poor. Their **per capita** income, or average individual income, in 1990 was about $360. The per capita income in the United States then was about $19,800—over 50 times as great.

The people of Croix Fer live in houses with dirt floors and without running water or electricity. They rise early, and every family member has chores to do before eating a breakfast of coffee and bread. There may be a piece of meat to eat a few times a month, but there is not much else to break the monotony of cornmeal and cooked greens.

The people of Croix Fer grow their own vegetables and fruit but often do not have enough money to buy soap to wash themselves or charcoal to cook their food. "I am hungry," is one of the most common phrases spoken by children just learning to talk and by old people no longer trying to hide what they feel.

Most people in Croix Fer do not have adequate medical care. The lack of medicine, of nurses, and of education about basic health care means that, before they are one year old, one-fourth of the babies die. Many people suffer from tuberculosis and other diseases that could be easily cured with the right treatment.

Like the people of Croix Fer, many rural families in the Dominican Republic live in mud-plastered huts without running water, above. Children line up with their buckets to wait for water at a public tap in a Port-au-Prince slum, below.

A Haitian family plants black beans—bought with a loan from the Inter-American Development Bank—on their small farm.

The people of Croix Fer work hard for their meager living. There is not enough good land on Haiti on which to plant the corn, sugarcane, and vegetables that they eat or sell. Neither is there enough pasture for their donkeys, cows, and goats. Their farms are rarely more than 10 acres (4 hectares) of very poor land; the average farm in the United States is almost 500 acres (200 hectares). Even if the people of Croix Fer could buy machinery, the tiny size and inaccessible location of their hillside fields would prevent the use of tractors.

In order to supplement their inadequate crops, the people of Croix Fer continually search for other sources of income. Many of them cross the border into the Dominican Republic in search of jobs as servants, masons, or tailors. A few people in Croix Fer smuggle goods across this border to make a little money.

Although there is little work to be found, many young people travel the long road to Port-au-Prince, the capital of Haiti, to look for jobs. Although it is now very difficult, a few have even traveled to the United States to

These women have come to Port-au-Prince to work in a clothing manufacturing company.

work as migrant agricultural workers. While they were in the United States, these people considered themselves fortunate, for in a few months they could earn many times their incomes from the fields of Croix Fer. When they returned home, they had enough savings to buy sewing machines, radios, or other goods that many of the people in Croix Fer want. Unfortunately, they also grew impatient with their quality of life and desired even more **consumer goods**. Furthermore, although the wages these migrant workers earned in the United States were much higher than they could earn at home, they were below the **minimum wage** in the United States. To keep employers from breaking minimum-wage laws and because of a growing anti-Haitian feeling in the United States, Haitians are no longer permitted to work in the United States.

Working Their Way Out

The people of Croix Fer, like poor people all over the world, want a better life. Their first wish is for more comfortable houses—houses with cement floors and several rooms furnished with beds, transistor radios, refrigerators, gas stoves—things that people in the United States take for granted. And if they dream wildly, they want an automobile or a vacation in Cap Haitien or the United States. These people realize, however, that to have these things they must make more money.

To raise their incomes, the people of Croix Fer need some **capital**, or money saved up. They could make a great deal of money raising pigs, if they were able to buy a few sows, or female hogs, and a boar, or male hog,

Few Haitians own cars, so most public vehicles get piled high with people and goods.

Market day in Port-au-Prince crowds the streets with stalls and sellers, while in the background a huge ship brings either tourists or imports—both necessities in Haiti.

to get started. With a little money they could build a pig pen and fence.

But the incomes in Croix Fer are very low. The people spend 80 percent or more of their incomes just on food. They rarely have any money left after they have fed and clothed themselves. The people of Croix Fer cannot save to accumulate the money to get started in pig raising. They are caught in a vicious cycle of poverty.

Economic development, which would break this cycle, is one of the major tasks facing poor people everywhere. Over the past 30 years, economists have tried to understand the patterns of development and social change. Why do some people have so little food, shelter, and running water? Why is this lack so widespread? What are the options that these people have for their lives? What is the relationship between poor countries and affluent countries?

These are very difficult questions to answer. They involve many complex issues and most are open to considerable debate among economists. The societies of the undeveloped countries differ vastly from each other and from those of industrialized countries. Quite frequently, when the causes and effects of development are studied, people in developed countries are influenced

In a rural classroom in Haiti, a teacher lectures his students on agricultural methods.

by their own wishful thinking. They see the world the way they want it to be or the way their societies operate, rather than each society the way it really is.

Usually, the development of an entire country, not just areas within the country, is studied. Economic development for a nation is usually understood as improving the ability of that country, as a whole, to manufacture goods, trade with other nations, raise crops, and generate electricity. In general, economic development means increasing productivity and wealth at all levels of the economy. Development also focuses on the improvement of social conditions and involves distribution of goods and wealth as well as such necessary services as education and health care.

A country's economic and social development are tied into each other. For example, a **cooperative enterprise**, such as hog-raising, would improve the living standards of many people in Croix Fer. Educating the children there would enable them to become more skilled and productive farmers and hog producers. Thus education and other social services are a part of development.

Seen broadly, development involves economic, political, and social conditions and choices. Ideally it is the process by which human communities strive to achieve a basic level of material goods, social services, and human dignity for each individual.

The achievement of human dignity is harder to describe than economic growth. Human dignity involves not only access to the necessities of life, but a certain measure of control over and security in one's individual destiny. We should not ignore this important part of development just because it is hard to measure.

COMPETING THEORIES
OF DEVELOPMENT

W hy are most people in Croix Fer and much of the Southern Hemisphere poor? Why are most people in the United States and much of the Northern Hemisphere relatively affluent? Different people give different answers. And the different answers have profound effects on people all over the world.

You can decide which answers offer the best solutions to the problems of underdevelopment in places like Croix Fer. At the same time, you might consider

the idea that most of the United States and much of the Northern Hemisphere is overdeveloped. The question is, therefore, who has the best explanation for under-development and possible overdevelopment?

Economists who study development have three general viewpoints, or theories: modernization, dependency, and alternative theories. They are based on different ideas about human nature, what governments should do about development, and how decisions about development should be made. A discussion of these three viewpoints will help you to begin to choose the one you find the most convincing.

Modernization Theory

In the 18th and 19th centuries, western Europe and the United States changed from being rural, agricultural societies to being urban, industrial societies in what is called the Industrial Revolution. Before industrialization, most people lived on farms and grew the food and made the products that they needed to live. During the Industrial Revolution, many people moved to cities and worked in factories to manufacture products that other people needed. They were then paid the money to buy the products that they needed. Most countries that experienced the Industrial Revolution are now affluent. Modernization theorists believe that less-developed countries will go through the same process of development—industrialization—that western countries did. The economic differences between the North and South will be reconciled as the less-developed countries become affluent.

Immigrants from _rural Europe_ crowd the streets of New York in search of jobs and a better life during the Industrial Revolution.

Modernization economists base their world view on the ideas of pioneer economists Adam Smith and David Ricardo. Like Smith and Ricardo, they believe that humans need positive reasons, such as wage raises, and negative reasons, such as threats of unemployment, to produce. **Capitalism**, an economic system based on private ownership and individual profit, and **free trade**, or trade without restrictions, are the best ways to promote development. They believe that development comes by leaving people alone to compete and maximize their individual profits. To modernization economists, economic development comes about automatically by allowing individuals to act freely and rationally in an open-market system.

Adam Smith (1723-1790) believed that the unregulated market, where people followed their own interests, created the most economic good for the most people.

A few modernization economists think that governments should not interfere in economic affairs. They believe that, left alone, the private market system will allow the most people to achieve the most good from the economy. The state, or government, should help keep enough law and order so that capitalism can operate freely. These economists are sure that many national and international economic problems are caused by government interference. They have one basic answer to the problems of poverty and underdevelopment: reduce

Left: *David Ricardo (1772-1823) thought that, in a fair trade environment, international specialization and division of labor between rich and poor countries helped both.* Right: *John Maynard Keynes (1883-1946) felt that some government spending was necessary to counteract the negative effects of the monopolies that developed under **laissez-faire** capitalism.*

government regulations and allow the free actions of individuals in the marketplace to make people everywhere better off.

At this time, most modernization economists think that the governments of rich countries can and should help the poor people of the world. Not many economists had this view until the Great Depression of the 1930s. Faced with global economic crisis, many economists came to agree with John Maynard Keynes. They saw that an unregulated economic system did not always fix itself. Keynes thought that governments would have to borrow and spend money to prevent economic depressions. Although they said that government should intervene to avoid economic depression, Keynes shared a strong faith in the capitalist system with other liberal economists.

A growing majority of modernization economists now feel that equality and social justice, rather than individual gain, are important goals. They accept the fact that government legislation and programs are necessary to achieve these goals. These economists are sometimes critical of the fact that the wealthy and powerful have greater opportunities. They agree that governments ought to tax the wealthy to help the poor and thus speed up economic development.

Some modernization economists also feel that poverty on the national and international levels has two major causes. One cause they cite is the tendency toward **monopolies**, or one company's control of a particular product or service. Monopolies, combined with too little or faulty government programs, are as much to blame for economic undevelopment as any inherent failures of poor people. These economists think that governments ought to intervene on behalf of poor people whenever the free market fails to provide basic human needs such as housing, health care, food, and adequate income.

Most modernization economists, agreeing with David Ricardo, also feel that world poverty can be eliminated if poor countries participate more in world trade. They feel that poor countries should make products that require a lot of human labor. These poor countries could then trade the goods they produce with their abundant labor for more sophisticated technical goods produced in the wealthier countries. According to modernization thinkers, such trade would help both the poor and the richer countries. In a free trade situation, each country could make the best use of its natural resources, capital, population, and technology.

Dependency Theory

Most economists in the developed world accept modernization economic views. In recent years, however, economists in less-developed countries and a few economists in developed countries have begun to question the basic assumptions of the modernization theories. These new dependency economists feel that humans are naturally productive and cooperative and are not motivated only by individual profit. They think that people can overcome both cultural and environmental obstacles to development.

Dependency economists believe that poverty cannot be eliminated in a world where the majority work hard to produce goods—the wealth of the world—that they don't keep, and where power remains in the hands of a few. Many argue that economic systems that pursue profit as their primary goal will never meet the basic human needs of the majority of the world's people. In fact, most dependency economists claim that national governments usually serve the interests of the wealthy few rather than the majority of the people.

These economists argue that the poor produce much of the world's wealth, but this wealth unjustly goes to the rich rather than benefiting the poor. Many dependency economists argue that if poor people have to work six hours a day to obtain enough money to live on, then any additional hours they can be forced to work for this same amount of money is **surplus value**. This is the difference

The government set up by "Baby Doc" Duvalier, above, in Haiti served only the wealthy elite. As a result, many poor Haitians emigrated to other islands in the Caribbean or to the United States.

between the value of a product and what the worker is paid. When there are lots of poor people in a country or a lot of poor countries in the world, poor people can easily be forced to produce surplus value for those controlling the land and factories.

Dependency economists base their argument on the belief that capitalist economic growth encourages poverty rather than eliminating it. They say that the development and expansion of Europe, progressing to the United States, Canada, Australia, New Zealand, South Africa, and Japan, caused the poverty of people in other parts of the world. The dependency economists believe that the natural resources and the labor of the ordinary people of Africa, Central and South America, and Asia made a few people in the industrialized nations wealthy. An even smaller number of elite in underdeveloped countries became rich also. By being forced to sell their labor at minimal levels of pay, the world's poor grew more alienated and miserable.

Alternative Theories

Alternative theories of economic development have evolved in the past 20 years. Based on ideas from both the modernization and the dependency theories, other explanations and solutions have been offered for the South's dilemmas. Most of these alternative approaches focus less on how development or underdevelopment came to be and more on what development should be. A number of recommendations are based on current overdevelopment "problems" such as pollution and alienation.

Alternative approaches agree that poor people need to play an important part in planning their own development. These approaches call for development by local or **grass roots** organizations of poor people, rather than national or international experts and leaders. Furthermore, most alternative theorists argue that many of the development problems of the Third World are due to unrestrained industrialization. They say that appropriate development involves a significant deindustrialization of the mass-production economies of the North. They also feel that the introduction of self-reliant, small-scale technological systems in the South is important.

Alternative development economists assume that the world cannot continue to grow as it has until now. A few call for a reduction in the "standard of living" in the affluent countries, especially in the United States. They feel that the United States, with 6 percent of the world's population, should not be consuming 40 percent of the world's energy supplies. Many call for a slowdown in growth throughout the world economy to avoid massive long-term damage to the environment. Almost all alternative development theorists agree that production should be geared toward the interests of both local communities and the global natural environment.

Instead of focusing on how the South could become like the North, alternative development theorists look at the world as one interdependent unit. They focus on how the entire world could be made healthier.

In industrialized countries, pollution is one of the many problems of overdevelopment.

3

MODERNIZATION THEORY OF DEVELOPMENT

O bviously the wealth of the world is not shared equally among its people. The richest 10 percent consume 60 percent of the goods produced. How did the people living in rich, developed countries come to be so much better off? Why aren't the world's resources distributed more fairly?

Modernization economists stress problems that poor people have which hold back progress. These economists are unlikely to focus on problems caused by the

In Guatemala, a worker picks the red berries of a coffee tree by hand.

international economic system. Instead, they say that the backward cultures of poor people are a major cause of undevelopment. Many poor countries are in the tropics. Tropical soils are usually not very good for growing crops. Rainfall in many parts of the tropics is unreliable, and many human and animal diseases are found there. Even so, many tropical countries provide raw materials used in the developed world, such as iron ore, sugar, and coffee.

Unstable political systems, ignorance of science and technology, lack of individual effort, and cultural "backwardness" are all causes of underdevelopment, according to most modernization economists.

Until very recently, most people in the United States were not even aware of the great gap between their affluence and the poverty of most of the world. If they did think about this gap, their thinking was shaped by their own experiences. They had "made it" and, like privileged groups everywhere, they felt their successes were

In England, a farmer plows his field in neat rows using a tractor.

the result of their own virtues. They advised less fortunate people to imitate them. They usually felt that the gap between rich and poor nations would disappear as the people in the rest of the world learned more modern ways, like theirs, of doing things. Poverty would disappear as economic expansion enabled all nations to become more like the West.

After World War II, an ever-increasing number of African, Asian, and Central and South American countries took their places alongside developed countries. It was assumed that the economies of these Third World nations would develop following the lead of their western "big brothers." According to the modernization theories of development, all societies pass through certain predictable, universal stages of development. The initial or "traditional" stage is characterized by low productivity.

Political leaders are seen as interested only in maintaining control rather than acquiring the technological, organizational, and other resources necessary to increase production.

This initial stage is followed by a "transitional" stage or stages, in which tradition is forced to give way to new, "modern" values, types of organization, and technologies. The best-known portrayal of this transition was the notion of the "preconditions for takeoff." These were essentially seen as the same economic and political changes associated with the rise of capitalism and the Industrial Revolution in western Europe from the 17th to the 19th century. The developed or modern society, the final stage in these theories, as might be expected, looked very much like contemporary western society—the capitalist, industrial nation.

The first goal of modernization, according to this theory, is to lay the foundation for long-term development. To do this, it is assumed that developing nations will need assistance for some time from western public and private institutions. The World Bank, the U.S. Agency for International Development, Chase Manhattan Bank, Gulf Oil, and Union Carbide are among those eager to become partners in development by providing loans or establishing foreign **subsidiaries**.

During this process of economic growth, inequality between the rich and poor is expected to increase as it has in the West. If a country follows a capitalist strategy, the path to rapid growth is to "build on the best." In other words, start with those individuals, groups, cities, regions, and resources that are already the most developed or that already have advantages such as education, skills, wealth,

In Sudan, workers sort batteries at an assembly plant that was funded by the Overseas Private Investment Corporation, above. In Tanzania, the United States sponsored a rock-crushing plant to help build the Tan Zam Highway, right.

power, good location, and plentiful raw materials. The purpose of starting with "the best" is to get the quickest return for each investment, the most output for the least input, the fastest growth along the lines of least resistance. The result is both rapid growth and a great increase in inequality between people, between regions, and between cities and rural areas. Modernization theory is biased in favor of efficiency and against equality.

Modernization theorists believe that greater equality will come about gradually as the economy's output grows. This process is not immediate. But, in time, continued growth is expected to "trickle down," or spread, to poor people and poor areas. As the economy expands, agriculture and industry should produce more goods and increase trade between producers and outlying regions. Trade with international markets should also improve.

In Haiti, an elementary school—a public service for these young children—is under construction.

Consequently, employment opportunities should increase and wages should rise. Public services, from health and education to Social Security and rural roads, should also multiply. So long as growth continues, its benefits should spread more widely and deeply, maybe not equally, but bringing absolute improvements to all. This gradual spreading of benefits is the "trickle down" aspect of modernization theory.

For the ordinary people of Croix Fer, modernization theories are of little value. For them, needs must be met now, and the benefits of eventual "trickle down" are yet to be seen.

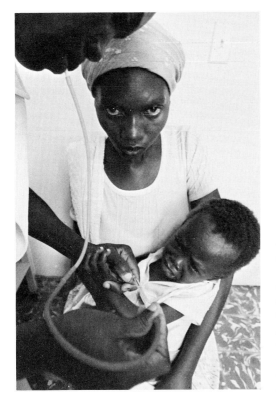

In Haiti, a lab technician at Sainte Thérèse Hospital— the first medical facility in the area— draws a blood sample from a 2-year-old to find out if he has an infection or is suffering from malnutrition.

DEPENDENCY THEORY OF DEVELOPMENT

After more than a quarter of a century of on-again, off-again immersion in the worlds of ordinary people in less-developed countries, dependency theorists find it hard to share the optimism of modernization theorists. Economic growth in this period has certainly not lived up to its promise in most of Africa, Asia, and Central and South America. The internal and external problems of underdevelopment seem greater than ever. A good number of less-developed

4

countries have faced stagnation or even decline in this period. Many rural areas seem to have gone backward in terms of quality of life. Growth has been more uneven and has generated even worse inequalities than those predicted by either modernization theorists or the historical experience of the West. The lives of the poorest—subsistence farmers, unskilled rural and urban people, the unemployed—are often getting worse. The number of people leaving rural areas for the cities, and of the urban unemployed, grows daily.

In the 1980s, hundreds of Haitians climbed aboard already over-loaded boats to make the perilous ocean journey to the coast of Florida.

A few countries have had "growth without development." The growth is shaky, the trickling down sparse, and dependency deepening. A small, privileged, "political" class has strengthened its economic position. Inequality grows. External assistance seems to create **trade deficits, balance-of-payment** problems, and **debt** crises. The indirect costs of dependency could be even higher: agriculture to produce goods for export uses up land needed for food production and the country's money is spent importing luxury goods for the few, in the midst of severe poverty of the many.

Dependency economists argue that underdevelopment of the South is not simply a matter of poverty. They feel that causes of underdevelopment do not simply lie within the country. They agree that the current difficulties of underdeveloped countries are not a temporary stage on the road to development.

To dependency theorists, poverty is only a symptom of underdevelopment—not a cause. As European countries colonized parts of Asia, Africa, and the Americas, capitalism, which was dependent on the underdevelopment of the colonies, developed in the "parent countries." The process, stretching from the 16th to the 20th centuries, resulted in slavery, exploitation, and loss of control over their own destinies for people in Southern countries. For the West, great wealth, industrial and military power, and domination of an expanding world capitalist system resulted. The South became underdeveloped through the exploitation that helped the West develop.

Western development was greatly assisted by cheap resources, cheap labor to extract or produce them, and protected markets in the colonies. An "unequal partnership" was imposed, helping the industrialized partner but harming the colonized partners.

Dependency theorists argue that less-developed countries are still politically manipulated, economically controlled, and culturally imposed upon by developed countries. International cooperation is regarded as just another way to keep what had been colonial countries under western control. The West continues to need both the natural resources and the consumer markets of the entire world. The development aid that the West gives or lends to countries of the South is bait that keeps the wealthy political elite in former colonies involved in the game. The aid costs the West little or nothing. In fact, countries of the West profit from the **interest** on the loans they make to less-developed countries. The total

In Ecuador, coffee beans are spread out to dry on a large, empty patch of ground in front of a stand of banana plants. Both coffee and bananas will be exported to the United States.

of all **transactions** between the producers of raw materials—the borrowers—and the producers of manufactured goods—the lenders—works out to a clear advantage for the developed countries. The results for the Third World are dependent economies and economic disparity within the countries.

Dependency theorists insist on a rethinking of the modernization approaches to development. Modernization theories make economic growth the chief goal. But dependency theorists say that economic growth and

In Guatemala, a farmer sprays pesticides on his onion crop, which will be exported to the United States.

modernization, within the developed world and in the international trade systems, increase underdevelopment in the South. The major goal of dependency economists is not economic growth. It is **egalitarianism**. They see economic growth as harmful unless it is linked to equality. The stages of economic growth defined by modernization theorists are regarded by most dependency theorists as a myth, at least for the South. Dependency and inequality on a world scale are not passing stages, but are built into the system which developed the North while underdeveloping the South. The stages of development do not apply to the South because external forces now determine the character of economic change in these countries. The modernization theories of development are replaced by theories based on liberation from western domination.

Dependency theorists call for a strategy of interreliance between less-developed countries. They argue that freedom from external economic control by the North is necessary for real development. This means controlling, if not forbidding, the introduction of external capital and consumer goods, especially luxuries. The door to the North should be guarded, even closed, to the extent that this is possible. Agriculture should be redirected toward producing food for local people or for export to other less-developed countries in the region, rather than toward crops that would be exported to developed countries. Industry should provide consumer goods needed for the people in the country rather than for export. Basic health and education services should be provided for ordinary people rather than only for the small economic elite, those who have political power.

This Jamaican uses straw to make baskets for local use instead of for export.

Cooperation with the North should take place only as a form of **collective bargaining** between equals. The present unequal partnership should be rejected. Only in this way, according to the dependency theory economists, can a new, more just world begin to emerge.

Putting Theory into Practice

It is difficult to say how dependency theory might affect the lives of the people of Croix Fer. The government of Haiti has not pursued a consistent policy of development. It seems to follow the path of least resistance, allowing **private enterprise**—international and domestic—an open field out of weakness and corruption. The results seem to support dependency theory's criticisms of the worst aspects of modernization theory.

Between 1972 and 1980, the government of the neighboring island of Jamaica did pursue a development policy

As in Jamaica, education systems to help people to read and write
have been set up in many other countries, such as Bolivia, above,
and India, below.

based on the principles of dependency theory. In 1975, 53 percent of the land in Jamaica was owned by only 1,000 people. The government established a land reform program that allowed 24,000 poor rural people to own farms by 1977. In a country where unemployment had passed the 25 percent mark, the government created 25,000 street-cleaning jobs in the capital city of Kingston. A minimum wage of 20 Jamaican dollars a month was established in October 1975. In this period between 1972 and 1980, the Jamaican government was successful in helping the five million people who could not read or write. In the first two years of the literacy project, 49,000 people were in class and 18,000 had learned to read.

After 1980, a new government in Jamaica returned to the modernization model. Not enough time had passed to test the results of using dependency theory to shape government policy for small farmers and agricultural workers in Jamaican towns. Pressure from lenders in the United States and the International Monetary Fund forced the government of Jamaica to **balance the budget** instead of focusing on the food, health care, education, and housing needs of the poor. It appears that, given international government policy, escaping from dependency is not easy.

5

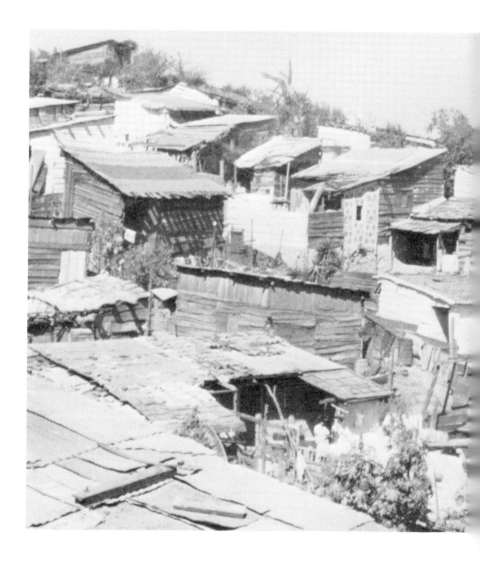

ALTERNATIVE THEORIES OF DEVELOPMENT

L ess than 100 miles (160 kilometers) from Croix Fer on the outskirts of Port-au-Prince, thousands of people live in squatter settlements. These people, with experience in small-scale farming, are unable to use their agricultural skills because they cannot find even a small plot of land on which to make a living. They live in unbelievably squalid conditions—families of six or eight living in a single-room structure about 10 x 10 feet (3 x 3 meters) in size. Some of these structures are shacks with walls of various wood pieces and roofs of corrugated iron. And others are shacks made of cardboard. All of the squatters live without regular incomes and without such basic services as water, plumbing, and education.

Standing in a Port-au-Prince squatter settlement, you can see some of the finest hotels in the country. It would be hard for those of us from affluent countries to be at ease with such obvious wealth amid such terrible poverty. But this contrast between poverty and wealth in Port-au-Prince is merely the world in microcosm. What is true for Port-au-Prince—an island of privilege amid an ocean of poverty—is true for the world as a whole.

In Rio de Janeiro, Brazil, luxury skyscrapers line the beach.

A fundamental fact is that most people of the world are poor and very little is being done to actually improve their quality of life.

Many people who have lived and worked in less-developed countries have grown impatient with economists who cling to both modernization and dependency theories. Their debates and the resulting governmental policy have done little to improve the lives of the poor people in Haiti and the rest of the South. There is an immediate need to create development practices that will rapidly improve the social, political, and economic conditions of the world's poor. For most poor people, it

In most of Brazil's cities, many people—often those who have fled rural poverty—live in slums.

Sponsored by a church instead of a government, construction workers complete the roof of a community building in one of Central African Republic's small towns.

has made very little difference which theory they or their national governments have accepted.

Most economists agree that trade between countries of the North and those of the South has usually been more profitable for the North. Dependency theory predicts that the less dependent a country is, the less it is likely to be exploited by other countries.

On the other hand, most economists also agree that many Third World countries do not have enough resources to be totally self-reliant—self-reliance is more or less impossible. A majority of economists accept the fact that aid directed against hunger, poverty, and desperation is needed in much of the South. Some economists feel that it might be necessary to link this aid to internal changes in the Third World, by tying it to specific projects designed to help the poor. These specific projects should not necessarily be in cooperation with national governments of industrialized countries.

Experience over the past three decades causes some economists to draw two conclusions:

1) Concepts, policies, theories, and patterns of development borrowed from developed nations and the transfer of technology from these nations tend to make developing countries less independent and self-reliant.

2) Developing countries have to fashion their own economic policies to address their own needs, problems, resources, and experiences. This does not mean that they can develop entirely on their own. But it does mean that they need genuine interdependence among less-developed countries rather than aid that increases their dependence on the developed world.

Alternative development thinkers are convinced that the world faces growing revolution or **repression** unless new economic patterns are created. Social justice and self-reliance should be promoted along with growth. For dependency and alternative development theorists, a world where people can interact in dignity as equals, both within each country and between countries, is necessary for human survival. Badly unbalanced economies lead to conflicts, which threaten world peace.

There is no single source for an alternative theory of development. But some common ideas are beginning to be widely shared by people directly involved in development with the world's poor.

One of these ideas is that the high production/high consumption development models followed by Japan, Germany, the Soviet Union, and the United States might not be best for the South. The United States continues to direct its economic efforts to further increase its own standard of living. Obviously in the Third World, where most people live at less than minimum levels of consumption, increases in production are necessary to ensure basic necessities for all. But even more important is fair distribution of what each nation produces. There is a big difference between production and consumption to meet social needs and the overdeveloped "pursuit of affluence" of the North. As Mohandas Gandhi put it, "There is more than enough to meet human need but not enough to meet human greed."

The Earth's resources have limits. The world cannot afford more economies, like that of the United States, based on overconsumption. Furthermore, though economists usually do not address such questions, the people of the South ought to question whether affluence ensures human happiness. Some thinkers in the North are questioning the value of unlimited growth from an ethical point of view. Experience indicates that affluence only makes people want even greater affluence. It does not necessarily lead to social or individual well-being.

Another premise that is widely shared among alternative theorists is that social justice has to accompany growth. The tendency for modernization to aggravate economic inequalities does not seem to resolve itself. A small, affluent group typically controls the means of production and political and economic power. This group becomes richer and more powerful, while increasingly

Material possessions, such as these houses in Australia and these cars in Great Britain, are what people in industrialized countries strive for. Do these possessions ensure human happiness?

At a nursery in the Dominican Republic, a worker tends tree seed-
lings until they can be planted. The resulting woodlands are useful
both to the Dominican economy and to world conservation efforts.

A Dominican worker stacks newly made athletic shirts for export to industrialized countries.

heavy burdens are imposed on the poor. This increasing unfairness causes serious social and political discontent, which in turn slows down development efforts and reduces economic progress.

Investment in social justice does not take resources away from an economy. Rather, money spent on education, public health, and housing increases the capacity of people to produce. People are the most important factors of production. In the long run, slum clearance helps an economy more than building luxury hotels. Increases in spending for education boost a society's quality of life more than the expansion of luxury goods production. Better health care programs are more valuable to a society than casinos. And small, viable community projects are more useful than prestigious sports stadiums and presidential palaces.

Poor people cannot buy very much. An economy that keeps most of its people out of the market stagnates. The affluent few soon satisfy their basic needs and then turn to suppliers outside the country for luxury

In Senegal, the grain sorghum is grown in large amounts. Bags of sorghum are sewn shut at the dock before being shipped to Mauritania, a country in the same region of Africa that is suffering from severe drought.

goods. Such a consumption pattern makes the South dependent on the North and the North dependent on the South.

Finally, a growing number of alternative development economists realize that, without major changes in the structure of the world economic system, development in less-developed countries is impossible. Most economists tend to shy away from political questions. But to plan and to push through these necessary governmental changes involves political decisions and new social and economic policy.

Multinational corporations that invest in Third World countries operate to earn profits. They owe allegiance to a few major **shareholders** rather than to the people of the developing countries they enter. The impact of these firms increases inequality, unless the government works to assure that resources are wisely allocated for the good of the whole society.

Experience has taught some of those who are directly involved in development projects among the world's poor the following:

- Development is a human-centered process. Technology and organization should serve the needs of people rather than the other way around.
- Participation of people in making and carrying out decisions is a major part of development, not simply a means to development.
- Self-reliance and cooperation, rather than rigid division of labor and dependence, are the basis for development.
- Development strategies should give highest priority to meeting the basic needs of all people, rather than providing more luxuries for the rich.
- High levels of consumption are inconsistent with development because they are out of reach of most people.
- All countries, rich as well as poor, have some development needs.

6

COOPERATING FOR CHANGE

People in underdeveloped countries remain almost completely dependent on foreign aid to finance any development project. Most of the more than 200 foreign aid organizations active in Haiti used the approaches of modernization theory, and were of little help to small communities like Croix Fer until recently. The vast majority of Haitians remain illiterate, hunger and disease are still widespread, and **life expectancy** in Haiti continues to be the lowest in the Western Hemisphere.

Because of the lack of success of foreign aid so far, it is crucial that alternative methods continue to be attempted. Alternative ideas about development are not just theories. They have been successfully tested in a number of places in the Third World.

In Mali, the easing of some government restrictions has allowed people to grow surplus crops, which they trade in the market.

On Haiti's arid northwestern coastline lies Coridon, a community with a population of 6,000. The Coridon villagers, **UNICEF**, and a few dedicated Haitian officials worked cooperatively to build a 10-mile (16-km) pipeline to supply safe drinking water to the village. The total cost of the pipeline was about $11 per person served. This initial success stimulated other community-based projects in Coridon. Funds were raised locally to fix the dilapidated school building, and some **reforestation** efforts have even begun.

Many grass roots initiatives like this around the world remain little more than "drops in the bucket." But as national and international alliances are built, the impact of alternative development plans will grow. In the long run, ways need to be found to transfer more land and capital to the poor. Dependency theorists' suggestions

Even large farms in Mali still use oxen for planting and harvesting crops.

about moving foreign and government spending away from the rich people in poor countries and ending the discrimination against everything that is non-Western and **indigenous** seem necessary. At the same time, the North should increase the flow of real resources to the South. Real resources would include supplying useful technology—irrigation systems, health care, more productive farming methods—and volunteers to teach the technology in ways that the societies could implement it. Real resources would mean leaving the southern countries alone, economically, to pursue their own development.

People who are searching for alternative theories of development find modernization theories of development of little use. They feel that the chief blocks to development in Africa are the low levels of education and agricultural technology. In Asia, overpopulation and unbalanced social systems condemn most people to landless poverty. In Latin America, the principal obstacle to development appears to be political systems that maintain very great inequalities. Without some attempts at grass roots development, we face a world of revolutions, dictatorships, stagnant economies, perpetual wars, and civil wars—a world very much like ours now.

GLOSSARY

affluence—An abundance of property or wealth.

balance-of-payment—A summary of the international transactions of a country over a period of time, including commodity and service transactions and capital transactions, in which they are equal.

balanced budget—A budget in which the government's income and expenses are equal.

capital—The value of a stock of accumulated goods.

capitalism—An economic system in which most industries are privately owned and operated for profit. Also called private enterprise, free enterprise, or free market.

centrally planned economy—An economy in which the allocation of goods and services is controlled by the government.

collective bargaining—Negotiations between employers and workers' representatives, usually unions, toward agreement on such things as wages, hours, and working conditions.

consumer goods—Goods that directly satisfy human wants.

cooperative enterprise—An organization owned by and operated for the benefit of those using its services.

debt—The amount of money a government has borrowed, minus the amount of money it has repaid.

economy—The total of all factors that affect the production, sale, and distribution of goods and services.

egalitarianism—A belief in human equality, especially with respect to social, political, and economic rights and principles.

free trade—International trade without restrictions.

grass roots—Society at the local level, especially in rural areas, as distinguished from the centers of political leadership.

indigenous—Having originated in and being produced, growing, living, or occurring naturally in a particular region or environment.

industrialization—The shift from manual to mechanized production of goods.

interest—The charge for borrowed money, usually a percentage of the amount borrowed.

laissez-faire—An economic ideal in which there is no government intervention in economic affairs.

life expectancy—An expected number of years of life based on statistical probability.

market economy—An economic system in which prices are determined by the buyers and sellers.

minimum wage—The lowest wage, as set by a government, that is allowed to be paid.

monopoly—A company that is the only seller of a good or service and therefore has considerable control over price and output.

multinational corporations—Large business firms with subsidiaries or branches in many countries.

per capita—The total of something from a country, divided by the number of people in the country.

private enterprise—*See* capitalism.

reforestation—Renewing forest cover by planting seeds or young trees.

repression—Putting down by pressure or force.

shareholder—Someone who owns a portion of property, such as a business or a piece of land.

subsidiary—A company that is controlled by a larger corporation, which owns the major portion of the subsidiary's stock.

surplus value—The difference between the value of the goods workers produce and their wages. In a capitalist economy, this amount goes to the private owners of the means of production.

sweatshop—Factories where workers are required to work long hours for low pay under harsh conditions.

trade deficit—A greater amount of spending by a country than income received from other countries.

transaction—A business deal.

underdeveloped—An economy that produces less than it could, given its factors of production.

UNICEF—United Nations Children's Fund.

Above Port-au-Prince, workers terrace the mountainside to begin reforestation.

INDEX

ACKNOWLEDGMENTS

The photographs and illustrations in this book are used courtesy of: p. 2, Jean Pieri; p. 7, Nigel Harvey; p. 8, Wendy Bell; p. 9, Laura Westlund; pp. 11 (top), 12, 13, 14, 36, 37, 43, 45, 57, 60, 68, InterAmerican Development Bank; pp. 11 (bottom), 51, David Mangurian; pp. 15, 26, Kaufman and Maraffi; pp. 16, 56, United Nations; p. 19, Ward Barrett; pp. 23 (left), 33, 48, Independent Picture Service; pp. 21, 22, 23 (right), Library of Congress; p. 29, Environmental Protection Agency; p. 30, Leslie Fagre; p. 32, Pan-American Coffee Bureau; p. 35 (top), OPIC; pp. 35 (bottom), 39, Kay Chernush/Agency for International Development; p. 40, U.S. Coast Guard; p. 42, John H. Peck; p. 46 (top), José Armando Araneda; p. 46 (bottom), Patrick Mendis; p. 50, Jim Cron; p. 52, American Lutheran Church; p. 55 (top), Australian Information Service; p. 55 (bottom), Wayland (Publishers) Ltd.; p. 58, World Bank Photo; p. 62, Piotr Kostrzewski; p. 63, Deborah Dyson; p. 72, Ron Regehr/Mennonite Central Committee, Akron, PA.

Front cover photograph courtesy of Nigel Harvey. Back cover photograph courtesy of Mitsubishi Motors Corporation.